DREAMS AND REALITY

VIKRAM BHARDWAJ

Made with ♥ on the Notion Press Platform
www.notionpress.com

Contents

Foreword

In this book, we are going to make some big claims - claims that are literally mind-blowing. We will try to prove these claims with logic, reasoning, and personal experience only. We will not be using any dogma, belief, or religious teachings. If you think that this particular thing or claim does not making any sense to me, you are free to question and even reject the claims. I believe that this book will change your life in the best possible way.

This book will be equally helpful to all types of thinkers and seekers out there: the agnostics, the atheists, the spiritual, the religious, and the neutral undecided person. Any seeker of truth who believes in his or her own knowledge and is not a blind follower of someone else will be greatly helped by this work.

We will also try to answer the most important question of human history: Who am I? What is the purpose of my life?

This question struck me in childhood when I was sitting idly . Suddenly my attention was drawn to ants walking in a long line like soldiers. Suddenly a thought struck me... what is the purpose of these ants? Are they just born to live and die like this, doing this stupid line walk? Then I suddenly thought, what is the purpose of a human life? Just live for a few years, experience circumstantial fun or pain, and then die? Thousands of people live and die each day. Am I also a part of this horde? Am I that trivial? Or is there a real purpose for my existence?

I didn't write this book to be an author. It's just that I wanted to get it out of my system. I have no interest in social service or being a guide or preacher. My reason is very selfish, or I could say SELF-ish. I just want to get rid of the itch to write about my experiences. If it helps anyone, good. I didn't receive any help while writing this. I just wrote what naturally came to my mind. That being said, let's dive straight into the deep end of the pool.

Prologue

DREAMS AND REALITY

You may be sure or unsure of anything in this world - why am I born into a rich or poor family, why am I sick with this disease, what's my fault, why do some people have cancer while people who smoke or drink daily for the last 40 years are having fun? Some people are born extremely lucky while some face problems at every step in life. Is there a God who controls this? Is the law of karma responsible for this? Is the law of attraction helpful to improve my situation? Is there a heaven? Will prayer or the so-called God help me? These are questions which confront us in our times of crisis.

You may accept or deny any such pattern of thinking/ belief but there is one thing which you can never doubt in this world – your own SELF. Can you deny that I exist? Nobody can. The denial of self itself proves the existence of denier's self. What is this "thing" I call "My Self" and why is it so important to know that? Our reasoning will begin with this fundamental question.

CHAPTER ONE

WHO AM I?

3:00 a.m: I saw my body. I am a lion, I am roaming in a jungle, watching countless animals. I hunt, I drink, and I copulate. I have a loving family. I rest in cool water, shooing away the flies sitting on my body. I feel proud to be the strongest animal, I shiver in fear at the sight of a hunter with a gun.

Somebody asked me - who are you? Me - Can't you see I am a lion, of course.

7:00 a.m: I saw my body. I am Vikram. I get up, take a bath, and get ready to go to college. I examine patients in clinics, meet my friends and my family. I attend my classes.

Who am I? Can't you see, man? I'm Vikram!

Both of these have been MY own experiences. Then who am I really?

Am I Vikram or am I a Lion?

If memory is considered as the criterion for reality, then I should be considered a lion. Because the memory of me being Vikram was not present during the dream state, but the memory of me being a lion was present in both the dream and waking state.

So why am I not a lion?

Who am I exactly?

The first big claim we are making is that I am neither lion nor human. I am neither in the state of dream nor in the state of waking.

In my own awareness, the waking world did not exist in the dream state. The dream world did not exist in the waking state. Both states were mutually exclusive and equally experienced. Waking is falsified in a dream, and a dream is falsified in waking.

So, do you mean that nothing is true? Both are false?

No, there is a truth. That truth is you. You were there when you saw yourself as a lion. You were there when you saw yourself as a human. You saw both the states of dreaming and waking. The states come and go, but you remain as a constant observer. That awareness or consciousness that you now call "I" is the real unchanging entity. You can deny or falsify both the states, but you can never deny your own existence.

There are a lot of radical claims here. These claims are weird, interesting but true. All you need to do is think over and decide for yourself.

1. Inside the dream, the dream world feels real. Inside waking, the waking world feels real.

2. But dream and waking states are NOT real. They definitely appear, they are surely experienced, but they are NOT real.

3. Dream and waking states both appear to the same underlying entity. This entity is the ultimate reality of these states as it is the only entity which is constant.

4. This underlying reality is the observer of these experiences. It is a conscious entity.

5. This underlying entity is the true Self (of lion, man or for that matter, any character that exists in those states). The lion may think of itself as an independent entity

running away from the hunter. But his identity and thinking are wrong. The self of both Lion and Hunter is actually the conscious entity in which the dream is appearing. Lion can't see the bigger picture. The real big picture is the consciousness in which the dream is unfolding.

6. These states of dream and waking are just passing through the consciousness like clouds in a clear sky.

7. This self is also the CAUSE of these states. The dream/waking universe arises, exists, and disappears in this entity. Anything that exists in the states is not separate from this entity.

8. This entity is SINGULAR. There may be a variety of things or events in this state, but all are one and the same because they all appear in that one conscious entity. Just like everything that exists in my dream is nothing but me. The train in my dream is me, the waterfall in my dream is me, and the music in my dream is me. Even the irritating fly in my dream is me. Singularity creates an illusion of multiplicity.

No doubt, I as a conscious entity experienced both the states of being a lion and a human. But just because I "experienced" something doesn't mean it's real.

In science, the definition of reality is something that can be experienced by the senses and is measurable and repeatable. But in OUR PARADIGM the definition of reality is not something we can experience, but something that is UNCHANGING.

I experienced being a lion and hunting a deer, but it was definitely not real. It was just an experience in consciousness. An experience in consciousness is not real; the consciousness itself is real in which the experiences arise, change and vanish.

So far these facts should be clear to everyone. Its a common experience of us all.

By the end of this book, you will be able to see a totally different paradigm of reality. It's not a theoretical intellectual gymnastics; it's absolutely relevant to our daily life. How and why, we'll see. This discussion will definitely lead to something interesting.

CHAPTER TWO

NATURE OF SELF

We have claimed that there is a conscious entity in which the waking and dream states appear and disappear. That consciousness is the Self of all entities existing in both these states (like lion and human).

We will spend some time analyzing this entity we feel as our own Self.

This conscious entity has unique inherent features which are not its properties or attributes but it just IS. Just like heat and light are not properties/attributes of fire, it's what fire IS. Without heat and light, fire doesn't exist at all.

1. This Self is not just aware of all other experiences but also aware of ITSELF. Just like light is used to see the objects in a room, but if you want to see the light itself, will you bring another light to see it? No, because the light has a unique quality of being self-luminous. This is just an example.

Suppose you are sent into a room and asked to count the number of people. You would say 7. YOU are needed to count the others. But if there is nobody in the room, just you, would you need anything elsc to know if you are there or not? Do you need any camera, scientific theory, or any wise man to know whether YOU are in the room?

No. Do you need to touch yourself or look at yourself in a mirror to confirm if you are present here? No. Because you are a SELF AWARE CONSCIOUS entity. Consciousness is by nature Self Aware.

2. This Self is Infinite, Consciousness, Bliss and Knowledge.

a. Consciousness – All experiences come and go, but we are aware of them. Things and events are all experienced by us. Without consciousness, there is no experience possible. Nobody needs advice from a prophet, text or scientist to tell us this. We are a conscious entity, and there is no doubt about it. If I doubt, that itself shows I'm conscious. Doubt can only arise if we are a conscious entity.

b. Bliss - Our Self is the source of our bliss. This is a little difficult to grasp but the Self is the seat of the bliss we experience in our day-to-day life. Not everyone likes my favourite ghobhi ki sabji. They do not feel pleasure when they eat it. But I get so much bliss from it. Where does this bliss come from? From gobhi? Then it would have been felt by others also. But only I felt the pleasure. So it means the pleasure came from somewhere inside me. In a dream, if you have an orgasm, you feel the pleasure of the orgasm in the same way as in real life. Where does it come from? It was all an inside job. We wrongly attribute pleasure to external objects. In fact, pain is universal - a knife will give pain to everyone, a burn will hurt everyone. But the same object (rock music) doesn't give pleasure to everyone. Pain is external, pleasure is internal. You need an outside world to experience pain, but bliss can be felt sitting alone.

c. Knowledge – Our self is not an object of knowledge. It can never be known as we know everything else around us. Also, it is not a knower. It feels like it's a knower but it's beyond both. In a dream, Raju is looking at an apple.

Inside the dream, it looks like Raju is the knower and the apple is known but from the dreamer's perspective (the real self), both are just an appearance. So, what is this Self if not known or a knower? So the claim is - the self is not a knower(subject) or a known(object). It is the knowledge itself.

If you forget the glasses on your eyes and are frustrated looking all around, suddenly you realise – oh, the glasses are right here, sitting on my nose. I'm wearing them!! This flash of "knowledge" is the nature of the Self. The Self is knowledge itself. It is an abstract thing and very difficult to grasp. But we all feel its magic whenever it flashes in our day-to-day life. "OHH!! I got it!!"

3. The only place where you can experience this consciousness is your own self, within you. The whole world, animals and humans, appear conscious to you, but think again. We only INFER that they are conscious. We don't know they are conscious. No where else in this universe consciousness can be experienced other than our OWN self. Have you ever felt the consciousness of others? You may feel their emotions, attitudes, and activities. But you can only indirectly infer that they are conscious. No machine, instrument, experimental deduction, theoretical or EXPERIMENTAL physics can prove its existence to you other than your own self.

4. You don't exist in the waking or dream state. It's the opposite. These states exist in you, the consciousness. YOU are the reality of these states. Without you, there is no experience possible. Without you, there is no existence possible.

The world we experience is just a thought in the consciousness.

5. Consciousness has a unique quality of creation. Just like you can create a whole world in your daydream, and it appears real to the man in the daydream. You know it's a false world, but the man in your daydream cannot know it's false. For that poor fellow, it's all real.

This consciousness might sound like something mysterious, something mystical or something hard to achieve, but it's nothing like that. It's always available to us. In fact, it's our own self which we experience every second of the day.

Please think about it and let's move on.

We will go on to discuss why these claims have a profound practical impact on our life, so much so that it is utmost important to know our true self.

We will also discuss and establish why life would be full of misery and suffering despite achieving all possible materialistic and worldly things, IF WE DO NOT KNOW OUR "SELF".

CHAPTER THREE

WAKING WORLD IS EXACTLY THE SAME AS DREAMING WORLD

The big claim of chapter 3 is that waking and dreaming states are exactly identical.

Just like a dream world arises and falls in our consciousness, so does this waking world.

In a dream, a whole world - situations, events and people - is created in consciousness. We feel like we are real person with real-life fears, happiness, anxieties, and pleasures. The time and space of a dream feel real. But when we wake up – the entire experience is falsified. The time and space are nullified. The personality and ego with which we were so strongly identified vanish in an instant.So do all the happiness, possessions and nightmares. In fact, they didn't even exist. Entire dream world was false, it just appeared but didn't exist.

Similarly, the waking world also arises in consciousness along with the entire universe and billions of humans and animals. Our personality in the waking world, our day-to-day life and events are exactly the same as in a dream. They appear real only in the waking state. They appear but don't exist in a real sense. They are as much as real or unreal as a dream world.

From the perspective of the dream state, dreams are real.From the perspective of the waking state, waking is real.

Let's call it BIAS OF STATES. That means when we are in a dream, we feel the dream world is solid, real and unquestionable. When we are in the waking world, we laugh at the dream state and say - waking is real. Or in other words, you may also call it the Power of The Present. The present makes the unreal look real.

We trivialize the dream just because we are analyzing it as a waking man from A WAKING STATE.

From the perspective of witnessing consciousness, there is no difference at all. Both dream and waking worlds appear and disappear just like clouds passing through a clear sky. All humans, including the one analysing these states, are just characters in a dream.

Once we TRULY wake up, the identity of lion/human is lost, and the reality of states is lost. Both states are falsified, and only the witnessing consciousness is left.

Now you could have multiple objections and questions to this claim (that the dream and waking are exactly the same).

Number 1: You could say that the dream world is vague and immaterial, but this waking world is real and solid.

If you break a wall in a dream, you will find bricks, cement and stone, not dreamy material. If someone shoots a bullet at you, it will be a solid, real bullet, not made of some cloudy stuff. During a dream, the world to a dreamer appears perfectly real and solid.

Number 2 – If you say that the dream objects and events are fake but waking objects have utility, think again. If you are thirsty in a dream, only dream water will quench your thirst, not a real glass of water lying on the bedside. In a dream, if you want to buy a burger, dream money will be useful, not real money. So dream objects are as useful in a dream as waking objects are useful in waking.

Number 3 – The dream world is not stable, this world is stable and continuous. Dream time and space is not real. Again, this is a bias towards your present state.

In a dream, the time and space feel totally real and consistent. The events in a dream feel real, stable and impactful.

Number 4 - Dreams "feel" hazy. Waking feels vivid. The first reason is the bias of state.In dreams, the world does look very vivid.As vivid as the waking world. Also, another important reason for this bias is that we are comparing our dream of the past (last night) with the present waking state. The present is by default always more vivid. Think about your lecture from 2 weeks ago. How vivid does it feel? It also feels hazy and "dreamlike". In fact, when we compare the dream to waking, we are comparing the "memory of the dream" to the present waking state. We should compare the past with the past.

However, the dream still leaves a memory in the waking state. The waking state does not even leave a faint memory in a dream. In fact, the dream would appear more stable than a waking state that way.

Number 5 – There is science in the waking state. I can check my dream state with EEG and sleep study. I have physical proof of a temporary dream state, and scientists can confirm my findings of being in a dream. But again, dreams also have scientists who would confirm a similar state in the dream world also. There is science, physics, and scientists in the dream world also who would uphold dream laws.

There are many other objections one can raise but there is no way you can prove IN YOUR OWN EXPERIENCE that these two states are not identical. Here you need to respect your own experience, thinking and logic.Dont look at anything other than your own Experience. What we are giving you are just suggestions to stimulate into a new level of thought. Explore them and the door will open to an an amazing new world.

So if we think logically, respecting our own personal experience without any bias, then we would have to agree that both the states of waking and dreaming are exactly similar when experienced from the present point of view without any past or future bias.

Now, since we have somewhat reached here, we would be making some more drastic claims.

Claim: time and space are not real. Only the observer is real.

Suppose in a dream you see yourself having a good life, elated holding your newborn son in your arms. You name him Arjun. You watch your son grow up and go on to become a billionaire. He takes you to Mars on his private jet rocket where he has built a brand new billion-pound mansion. You are standing on Mars and marvelling at the universe and distant galaxies.

Then you suddenly wake up. You were sleeping in your bed for the last 6 hours.

Can you deny that you had this experience of vast time and space spanning decades of years and millions of miles?

So if you consider yourself as a man sleeping in a small bed, how can a rocket, Mars, spacecraft, and Earth exist inside you?

Now you have to analyse your OWN experience and logic. You don't have to rely on anyone else here. What can we conclude from this experience - you were the dreamer, and a world with all its happenings appeared in you, right? It clearly shows:

1. You are not a small person sleeping in a room. You are the consciousness in which this entire experience - time, space, and events - appeared along with your own persona, Mr Arjun.

2. You don't exist in the waking or dream state. It's the opposite. These states exist in you.

3. Time and space exist in consciousness. Consciousness does not exist in time and space. In fact, consciousness can control time, space and events.

4. Time and space are not absolute reality. Observer or consciousness is the only absolute reality. In one hour of dream, you can experience going to Bali, having fun, and maybe a tragedy like an earthquake and come back to India - an experience of a lifetime may happen in an hour. For the conscious observer, time was not absolute, it changed - depending on the state that appeared in consciousness. Time and space contract and dilate in the presence of consciousness. That's why consciousness is a truly amazing entity.

5. Consciousness is infinite. Finite and infinite are concepts when we look at something from the perspective

of time and space. If there is an entity in which time and space themselves exist and vanish, that entity is beyond finite and infinite mess. I would like to call it SUPERINITY.

6. Where did the lion in the dream come from? Who were its parents? Did it evolve from fish and octopus on the way to becoming a lion? Is there evolution in a dream or just an appearance?

The world appears, it doesn't evolve. What came first? Egg or hen? Neither!! The observer came first. Consciousness came first.

7.The dreamer exists everywhere in the dream. In fact, the dream world is nothing other than the consciousness (dreamer). Everything in a dream (cars, trees, people, stars) is in reality the dreamer itself. In my dream I am everything. The car in my dream is me, the tree in my dream is me, the people in my dream are me, my personality in my dream is me, even the stars in my dream are me. I am omnipresent in my dream. Does a man existing in your daydream have a separate existence? Will you get an AADHAR card made for a man existing in your dream?

8. Dreamer knows everything in its dream. So in my dream, I'm All Knowing. I know all humans in my dream.

But a man in a dream can never know the dreamer. No matter how much effort a man may put in, he can never know the dreamer with effort. For a dream man, the dreamer is not achievable by effort but only by dissolving his identity.

9. In my dream, I can change anything. Suppose I'm daydreaming; I can make a cow fly in my dream. In my dream, I'm the All Powerful.

10. There is a single non-dual consciousness in the whole dream state. Every individual in the dream may appear conscious, but in reality, their consciousness is

unreal. There is only ONE CONSCIOUSNESS in which everything appears (and then disappears). There are no multiple conscious entities.

11.The individual inside the dream is stuck with his limited individuality until an amazing event occurs – waking up. When consciousness wakes up, there is no individuality remaining. Alternatively, it could be said that when individuality disappears, consciousness awakens.

12. There are two levels of reality dependent on the observer's "identity-bonding." The waking world is a lower level of reality, while consciousness is the higher, ultimate level of reality.

Now, all of this may seem very abstract and a foolish, impractical errand. What does it have to do with me? I must think of my children's education, my investments, my job and layoff, my joint pain and hearing loss. I'm not a professor of philosophy to waste my time on infinity , Self or consciousness stuff.

But, beware! This consciousness thing is the most important. In fact, everything else is immaterial compared to consciousness. Once you understand the meaning of this self, consciousness – everything else is trivial just like the circumstances of a dream awakened from.

This is the most practical and useful knowledge. It will be clear once we go through this discussion.

There is no Peace without this.

CHAPTER FOUR

HOW DOES IT MATTER IF THE WORLD IS REAL OR FAKE?

Now, you might say, "OK. Suppose I believe you for a moment, whatever you have said. Both waking and dream are false. Only my consciousness is the true entity in which everything is appearing temporarily."

So even if waking is like a dream, what is the problem in living in this world? I am having a good life. I have a good family. The life is going on smoothly. Why should I waste my time on this stuff? What's the problem even if this world is unreal like a dream?

The huge problem is this.

This waking state and the world which we consider solid and real are actually not real. They just appear stable and real at the present moment. They are temporary and short-lived.

But your true nature, the ever-existing consciousness, is permanent.

Temporary things can never satisfy the permanent.

That's the main reason.

Whatever you achieve in this world, the temporary cannot satisfy the permanent, especially when that permanent is also the seat of bliss. The permanent will always seek bliss; it will never stop. It will be an unending, unsatisfying hard work if we try to achieve bliss in the temporary existence.

The other reason is - the bad experiences will make you miserable.

Let me share my own experience (I realized and wrote it in 2020).

I was hit by COVID during the 2020 Coronavirus pandemic. I am a 37-year-old surgeon having achieved everything I have ever dreamt of in my life. Every year, I make a list of things/goals I want to have, and trust me, I had already achieved almost everything I wished for. Materially, professionally, spiritually, in my personal life, I have it all. I had seen it all from a poor village life in India to luxuries in Miami to Singapore. I had super fun with friends and family which most people can only wish for.

I always believed NOW I can die a satisfied man.

That was until COVID hit me.

I got sick and was admitted to hospital.

It was the first time I had ever been admitted or fallen seriously ill in my life.

But the strange and honest thing was, I was scared of dying. The fear of death and sickness made me think and reflect.

Although I have enjoyed everything life has to offer - I am generally healthy with no addictions, have a wonderful supportive family, healthy and happy parents, sufficient funds, and great friends...

So despite all this, why was I afraid and miserable?

The question troubling me was - Is there something which if ONCE achieved, doesn't make me miserable anymore? One happiness which overtakes ALL miseries? I have enjoyed everything but is there anything which gives **REAL AND PERMANENT happiness**?

Suppose a student who is very rich, driving in a Mercedes to his school, but he has not finished his homework. He is scared of being humiliated in front of the whole class.

Another student who is poor and coming on a bicycle is totally in bliss with joy bubbling inside because he has finished his work. He knows he is saved from scolding.

My question is - does the joy of sitting in a Mercedes take away the rich boy's misery and fear? If not, then what's the use of Mercedes? What's the use of riches or influence if it can't take away ALL your miseries?? Can thousands of pounds take away the pain of a wealthy man's incurable cancer? Can money avoid death and disease?

If a child falls sick, can his father become happy and joyous remembering the fun he once had over drinks with his friends? That lovely night at wildfire camp - will it give the worried father any solace when his child is in ICU?

Then doesn't it mean that all such pleasures are just TEMPORARY and meant to be for THAT moment only? What is the fun of collecting money/good times/world tours if they can't take away **ALL** your problems?

Is there something in this world that **ONCE ACHIEVED** takes away all present and future suffering? That is the quest. This is also the main quest of this book.

Suppose you are in a dream and someone cuts your hand. You would be extremely agitated and deeply miserable. You can imagine the pain and agony of such a state. How will this pain and suffering go? The first option is if someone performs a very great surgery and repairs your hand. The second option is if someone with a magic wand can just say abracadabra and repairs your hand.Would that make you permanently happy?

The answer is NO. None of the above.

In such a scenario, you would invariably develop an attachment and love towards the person who healed you, and hate towards the person who cut your hand. It would lead to further good and bad actions and perpetuate the cycle of cause and effect, action and reaction.

The only true and permanently effective method to erase the suffering is much simpler – **WAKE UP.** Waking up from the dream takes away all the sufferings of the dream - **instantly and permanently.** And more importantly, it's effortless.

The big claim of this chapter is that unless we realise and awaken into our true Self, we can never be happy and fulfilled. Both dream and waking state cannot satisfy us unless we WAKE UP.

Now your next question should be, "I Am not suffering at all in this world" I am very happy and doing pretty well in my life. Whatever you are claiming might be right, **but I have no suffering.** I'm chilling out and having a great time. EVEN IF IT'S A DREAM, WHY SHOULD I WAKE UP?

This is a lovely dream, let me enjoy it.

CHAPTER FIVE

THE LOVELY DREAM IS NOT ALL THAT LOVELY

The objects of the senses - wine and women, delicious food, amazing views on a great vacation, the lovely hospitality in resorts and restaurants, lovely clothes, thousands of social media likes and appreciations, fun with friends, etc. - these can never permanently satisfy you.

Material and sense pleasures are unreal and temporary. Let me show you why they are trouble and not a pleasure.

Number 1 - The effort to collect and maintain.

There is great hard work, stress, and mental anxiety, and even humiliation, to collect money and material objects. How much effort does it take to achieve a small material gadget? You work like a slave to fulfil your desires. You buy a house, but you will not be satisfied. You will work for a car, then you will work for a bigger house, then you will work for investments, taking out loans all the time.The cycle of materialistic collection and slavery will never stop.

Look at those poor people who don't even get food. The entire day, they work in the sun and rain just to earn a few rupees to have food. Look at the poor people doing manual jobs on the roadside. But they have to do this labour to obtain material things. Similar is true for a government or private employee. They work day and night, even when sick. Everyone has their struggles, even CEOs. People who don't have the attitude to be peaceful and satisfied will be miserable even if they are millionaires.

In fact, it is a cumulative effort. Things keep adding up. because once we achieve a nice house and car, we would want a bigger house and car. There is no end to the materialist world.

On the other hand, just being oneself is so easy and free of cost. If you just decide you do not want that iPhone, how much money, effort, and time would that save you? In school, I read a story in Punjabi called "boot di shararat" . It hilariously depicts how buying fancy shoes lead someone farther and farther into materialistic necessities.

Number 2 – Maintenance. Once you have gathered all the attractive objects in your pleasant and lovely abode, including your splendid car and reputation, it is even more stressful to maintain these things.

Whether it is money, health, or reputation, a person has to maintain the initial hard work and stress just to sustain their previous lifestyle. You have to keep up the original effort and more to just maintain your material achievements.

I know better than anyone. When I got admitted to MBBS with an All India rank in the top 100, my reputation was very good in front of everyone. In the first year of MBBS, I fell into bad company and influence and was on the verge of failing my exam. At that time, I was crying and praying - oh God please save me please help me I will lose my respect. Let me pass the exam this time. Next time I will work hard. I realised then that - it is an even bigger task to maintain your material positions and reputation after achieving them.

Number 3 – Effort to Enjoy.

After you have achieved and maintained the sense objects, you need healthy sense organs to enjoy them. You need a healthy body, a great physique. How many trips to the hospital, gym, cosmetologist, and doctor are required just to enjoy the sense objects? Excessive sense objects make us feel physically and mentally sick. Your senses must be in perfect state to enjoy the fruits of your hard work.

There will be a time when your body will be old and frail. You will be unable to use your sense organs. Eyes will be weak, hearing will be lost, even swallowing muscles become weak. You will have erectile dysfunction. The desire for sex will burn in the heart but the body will be too weak. I have seen many such old tharki buddhas (old horny men) who have sexual urges but unsuccessfully use Viagra. The body won't be fit enough to enjoy your exploits of hard work. What will you do then? Will you tolerate the sexual urge? No other option. Then why not control that urge now?

Number 4 - Sickness due to indulgence. Look at those super-rich people who have become sick while indulging in wine, alcohol and beautiful women. They get diabetes and become obese. Many become drug addicts. Many go into depression.

When I was doing my MD in Ludhiana, I had a rich friend who had inherited agricultural land, a famous restaurant and businesses. He was filthy rich. But every evening he would call me to hang out. Mostly, I refused because I was too busy. I realized at that time that the guy was very rich, but still he was dependent on me for his fun and enjoyment. He later fell into depression. How much alcohol and women can you enjoy, how many clubs and vacations can you visit? There is dissatisfaction in all of this after some time. Only truly rich people understand the limitations of money.

5. Senses will shroud your self. Sense activity drags you away from your true self, deeper and deeper into the dream. This is more of a problem from a spiritual aspect than a practical one, but it is crucial because that is what matters most in the end.

Knowledge comes in three types

Sense knowledge (indiya janit gyan) - generated through sense organs,

Mental or brain knowledge (buddhi janit gyan), and

Self-knowledge (atma Gyan).

Sense knowledge can be very misleading. You see a mirage - you saw water. But that is a totally false knowledge collected by eyes which perceives it as water.

You see a dream with a cow flying in it. It wasn't seen through any sense but through the mind only. But that dream is also not correct knowledge. There was no cow flying, but your mind created and experienced this false experience. So, buddhijanit gyan may also be false. However, atma gyan or Self-knowledge is never false. The sense pleasures work in a similar way.

Number 6 - In the world, we achieve things "one after the other". We work hard and hustle, then achieve a milestone. Then, we start another pursuit. We get a good home, finish the loan, but then we get a car, finish the loan. Then, we have kids and education, finish that. Then, we have their marriage and so on. And that keeps on and on until we die or get wise.

But when you wake up to reality, all achievements are gained INSTANTLY AND COMPREHENSIVELY. That's a very powerful state to achieve.

Number 7- Pleasure is not in the sense objects. If the pleasure were in sense objects, everyone would love the same things - the same classical films, the same food, the same hobbies, the same persons, the same friends. It's not like that. Pleasure is in the Self. Pleasure is not in the object. Pleasure is always inside us.

Suppose a person is having an orgasm in a dream. Where did that pleasure come from? There was no other human or sexual activity taking place but the pleasure was as good as real. That pleasure comes from inside. Pleasure doesn't need an outside object. There is a source of bliss deep inside us, which is both hard and equally easy to achieve.

The seat of pleasure is in the Self. In outward things, all we get is only a tiny reflection of the inner pleasure.

Number 8 - Sense pleasures are dwarfed by misery. Suppose Rajesh likes gulab jamun; he is crazy about it. He would never miss eating it no matter what, that's what he claims. Today, he got three gulab jamuns in front of him and he is ready to eat. Just then, he got a phone call - "Rajesh, your mum and dad have had an accident. They are in hospital emergency." Would Rajesh still want to enjoy that gulab jamun? No. He would leave behind his desire for gulab jamun and run for his parents. Is this what sense pleasures are worth? They lose their importance in an instant when confronted by misery.

Number 9 - It's an ancient saying in India – "Others are loved for the sake of Self". You don't love any random child, you love Your child. A husband loves a woman as a wife not because she is a person. He loves her because she is His wife. Before marriage, if the same girl is hit by a car, he won't be worried that much, but after marriage, the same girl would become so dear to him. Once the feeling of "mine" enters, then only the objects become dear. A billionaire has a private jet, but that gives me no pleasure because it's not mine. Without Self or Mine, nothing is dear or loved. Once you expand your identity to your Real Self, everything becomes Yours. And so does all the pleasure of everyone.

Number 10 - Life seems long, but it's very short and ephemeral. We may think that our life is very long and stable. But go back to our dream analogy. In a dream of 2 hours, we can see a life of 50 years or travel to different places.

Number 11 - There are few pleasures in life but there are countless troubles. Let's count the pleasures you can enjoy - family, health, holidays, wine, sex, compliments, friend's company. Now count the number of troubles you can get into - Covid, cancer, paralysis, dementia, legal case if you hit someone on the road, business loss, a tree falls on your head, lightning strikes, an earthquake destroys your home, loss of reputation, you are cheated, you are laid off, a mortgage pending, a family member bedridden... the list is endless. Just check the morning newspaper and compare the bad and good news. It's actually true that bad things are more frequent and varied than good events.

Anytime any bad thing can happen out of the blue. Life can change in an instant – rarely for good but usually for the worse. Good things take effort to get, bad things just come uninvited to topsy-turvy our world.

Ask yourself - What is it that you have not already enjoyed? You have money, you have freedom, you have cars, you have a girlfriend, watched movies, amazing food, amazing sex. So, what did you get? Are you satisfied? If you are so satisfied, what are you doing here reading this book? Have you loaded your Happiness Gun to shoot at the misery enemy? Are you Misery-ready for the future?

Tell me one such pleasure that does not give you guilt. Tell me one such pleasure that does not make you weak. One such pleasure that does not break your resolve. One such pleasure that does not make you sad and miserable.

Why are you making a fool of yourself? You know that sense objects can never satisfy. Same alcohol, same wine, same women, same music, same company, same situations - it's just a repetition again and again. As the gladiator asked the filthy crowd, "Are you not entertained?"

Momentary pleasures do not serve any practical purpose for a far-sighted person. You cannot use a momentary flash of lightning in the sky for your daytime routine. Flowers don't bloom in the momentary light of thunder. A man of wisdom or even a ruthless modern day achiever will have nothing to do with momentary streaks of pleasure. He knows that he can't bake bread with a matchstick fire.

Why not achieve something which stops this pain and pleasure once and for all?

If material possessions could have caused liberation, then we might have had an alternate world order. We work hard, with discipline, hard work and dedication to achieve material objects and wealth. After a certain threshold is achieved, we would be liberated and happy PERMANENTLY, immune to all disease, death and bereavement. But such an order or scheme of things doesn't exist. Does it? Steve Jobs had cancer, rulers and kings die.

If you still believe there is no misery in the world, you need a serious reality check.

You might be living in a beautiful jail.

But how strange human nature is.

You would see a person crying - Oh God, I am so miserable, please help me. I am stuck in this miserable disease or situation. "But still you would see the same guy running after the illusory world and frivolous things. Not after the true self consciousness. That's strange. This is called delusion of life.

It's actually not a philosophical thing. There is an actual illusion created by the mind which creates this delusion. It's all physics in the end. It's all because of the error created due to unique characteristics of this entity called Self or Consciosuness. We will discuss this illusion and error business in the coming pages.

How strange that the ocean of bliss and happiness is inside every conscious entity, yet every conscious entity is running after an unconscious material entity. How strange this is. How wonderful this is. How amazing this is. This is the glory of consciousness and the mystery of consciousness.

This chapter is basically for those great people who have already achieved some level of success and wealth in life. Only a wealthy person can appreciate the limits of wealth. For those who are poor and unsuccessful, they will not see the point over here. Spirituality is for people who are at a certain advanced level of life – emotionally, materially, and intellectually. Rest of the people are just roaming around to taste the basic pleasures of life. But India is lucky in this respect. Here, even the poor people have a sense of detachment and spirituality something thats hard to achieve.

CHAPTER SIX

LOCATING MY SELF

You may think, "What all fantasy thoughts we are thinking. I'm a surgeon/businessman, scientist/student. I feel weird thinking of these things, sounds like foolishness and time wastage."

But hold on. I would like to call them Thought Experiments to discover the greatest and most valuable treasure of the universe. I would like to call us all Spiritual Einsteins.

When someone asks me who I am, I would say I am this person with a unique personality and personal history, including my particular body and mind - whether good or bad, literate or illiterate.

But really - Who am I - the one who is experiencing this world. What is this entity I call "me"?

Am I this body? Am I this leg or hand? If my hand or foot were cut, would that reduce my sense of Self? Would my experience or feelings reduce if my finger was cut away? No. I say "my hand", I never say "I am the hand".

Yesterday, we went to the forensic department morgue. I saw a small body covered with a sheet. I thought, "So sad, it must be a child." But then the sheet was lifted, and I saw it was a grown-up man cut in half by a train.

That struck me and made me think: Suppose my body is cut in half in an accident and I survive somehow. Will the feeling of "I" reduce to half? Would my thinking, desires, personality, and intelligence also reduce by half?

Of course not. This clearly means I am not my body. The body keeps on changing. The body gets healthy, the body gets sick.

Sometimes it feels energetic or lazy. But I keep watching these changes in the body. Definitely, I am not this body. I saw my body when I was a teenager, when I had great hair. I saw my body when it was sick and when it was healthy. The body changes, "I" don't.

Am I this mind then? The mind is even more fickle than the body. The mind is always changing. Sometimes focused, sometimes wandering. Sometimes very spiritual, sometimes very materialistic. The mind is nothing but a series of thoughts. All sorts of thoughts arise and go - the good, the bad and the ugly. But I am always watching these thoughts. When we were young, we lived in a small village called Badrukhan in Punjab. Sitting on the Shiv Mandir wall, we could see the national highway in front of us. Occasionally a vehicle would pass along. Our game was - we would pick one side of the road. If any vehicle came from my side, I would punch my friend in his back. If a vehicle came from his side, he would hit me. These thoughts are like vehicles passing on; I'm just a peaceful spectator unless, of course, I start running after them, and then it's trouble. I am the witness of this ever-changing mind. The subject can never become the object. Since I'm watching the mind, I can't be the mind.

Am I the intellect which is the decision-making faculty inside me? The decisions keep on changing. Sometimes I don't understand a situation. And then suddenly, I get it! Even my decisions keep on changing. In the same situation, sometimes the brain decides this, sometimes the other way.

When I open a fridge and see a mango - sometimes I decide to have it and sometimes I decide not to have it. I can observe the changing, unstable decisions of the brain.So I am not this intellect either.

Am I this personality which I have known for so long? The person called Vikram? This ego I believe I am. This person has been changing right in front of me - from childhood with all its foolishness and games to adulthood with all its ambitions and desires. I am certainly watching this person who is changing for better or worse every day. Sometimes, I have a feeling of a superiority complex and sometimes feel guilty and inferior. I am certainly the observer of this personality or ego. It can't be me.

Then who am I?

Maybe I don't know - but at least there **is** something which I call "I". **There is something** which is experiencing the ever-changing world - body, mind, and ego. Right now, right here. You can doubt the existence of anything, any idea, any concept, but you cannot doubt one thing - your own existence. This "I" is right here, and you need no proof of this. You are your own proof.

If there were nothing at all, even the question "who am I?" does not exist.

The existence of the question itself justifies the existence of the Self.

Let us analyse your Self. Please do not believe anybody. It is your own personal experience, your own conclusion.

1. It is permanent. The Self is always there. In any situation, your Self never goes away.

The experience of this Self will be the same at 15, 50, or 90 years of age.

2. IT IS SELF-AWARE. You don't need any sense organ, any theory, machine or concept to know your self. If you are put in a sensory deprivation chamber , you will still be aware of yourself. . Even in deep sleep, you are still there. That's how you report - "I slept peacefully and had no dream."

3. Everything changes - the world, body, mind, and ego, but the self never changes. It is a witness of these changing states.It is unchanging.

4.It is bliss. Now, this is a little hard to grasp, but a simple observation is deep sleep. In deep sleep, there are no mind, no state, no thoughts, but still, we say "I slept peacefully. I am energised. I'M BLISSFUL".

5. The self is not in a dream, waking, or deep sleep state but these states are in the self. The world that we experience in our day to day life, exists in Self just like a dream world exists in Self. The material world is nothing but consciousness . If we can grasp this fact, it will be a paradigm shift in our day-to-day life.

6. The self is transcendent and immanent in the world. It pervades the world and still lies beyond it. Just like in a dream, the world is made of the dreamer himself, but the dreamer is still beyond the dream world. Nothing in the dream world can touch the dreamer.

7. IT IS AN INSIDE JOB. In fact, your own self is the only place you can find consciousness. Other people may feel conscious to you, but you have no way to confirm their consciousness. You can only indirectly infer that.

8. This is the existence itself. This is even harder to grasp: the claim that the entire world is appearing in consciousness and everything that exists is nothing but consciousness. In fact, consciousness is not an existing thing, it is **existence itself** (of all existence).

9. Whenever you try to experience this self, you will always find/experience a kind of peace and stillness. So it's peace itself.

10. The self is the subject which experiences everything.

But nothing can experience the self. It can never become the object of senses or mind. Balls in a box can never comprehend the box, but the box can fully comprehend the balls lying inside it.

11. When you look at a ball, the ball is known (object), you are the knower (subject), and there is some abstract but existing entity called knowledge. This self is not knower or known – it's the nature of knowledge.

Many aspects of this Self can be experienced by normal people – like awareness, existence. But its other aspects - bliss, knowledge, infinitude, stillness, omnipresence, omniscience, and all-powerfulness - are more difficult to grasp. They are felt by us when our mind fulfills three important conditions - it should be pure, introverted, and focused. Then the aspect of bliss, all-controlling, and omnipresence also become evident, which appear mystical to ordinary people.

CHAPTER SEVEN

HOW DOES THE WORLD ARISE IN CONSCIOUSNESS?

We understand that the ultimate reality is an entity that is Conscious, Infinite, Existence and Bliss. But if that's the reality, what is this world we're experiencing? Where has it come from?

This is the most debatable question with no clear answer. I'll just share my own personal understanding.

Suppose there is an entity which is conscious and also infinite. Now whenever such a conscious entity exists, by nature, it will experience something because its conscious. But there is nothing else in existence. Since it is existence itself (anything else other than existence is non-existence by definition and logic),

So it has no option other than to experience itself.

When a conscious entity experiences itself, it creates an ERROR e.g. if you are looking at yourself, you can't see the back of your head. Also, if you experience yourself in a mirror, you can't experience yourself completely. Even the eye cannot see itself. Only its reflection OR IMAGE can be seen. So a conscious entity trying to experience itself creates an ERROR. Technically, the reason for this error is that the subject can never be an object.

But this entity is also infinite. Infinity is, by definition, unknowable. So when a conscious entity tries to experience itself, which is also infinite, it creates an even bigger error.

Therefore, an error is created in the consciousness, by the consciousness, for the consciousness.

This error is time, space, and existence. So, it sort of creates an antithesis to itself. Being consciousness creates unconscious matter. Being timeless, it creates time. Being infinity, it creates space that can be compartmentalized. Being bliss, it creates suffering.

A combination of these elements - unconscious matter, time, space, suffering - along with a pinch of original reality creates a wonderful mixture called the world.

All these anti-Entity things we see in the universe are all an ERROR.

An unstoppable force hits an immovable object. What will happen? By definition, one is unstoppable and the other is unmovable. It means the question itself is wrong; it's an error. When a conscious entity tries to experience its own Self, which is Infinite, it causes an error. The subject creates an objective world which is an error. So this entity appears with opposite characteristics.

But even this error is bound by rules and laws. Since that ENTITY is INTELLIGENCE itself, the nature of knowledge, even in the erroneous universe, is RULES-BASED. I like to call this universe a NECKLACE OF ERRORS where time, space, gravity, laws of physics, planets, animals, etc. are PEARLS OF ERRORS held together in a rule-based order by the string of consciousness, infinite, blissful entity. And that entity is YOU yourself. We experience it as our own self, but it's so hard to fathom. It's nothing short of amazing.

Now you may not be satisfied with this explanation. There may be many other theories which may interest you. Debates are endless.

So, the entity exists in both states: an error state and a non-error state.

These things may sound very abstract, but there is nothing theoretical about this. This conscious entity is our own self. And without a true understanding of this self, we can never be happy, and we cannot stop and rest.

We will keep on running round and round with ups and downs like the Kohlu of old times. Further we are from the centre of this kohlu, the faster we have to run, the more difficult it will be to catch up. The nearer we go to this axis, the happier and easier we will be. Only when we grasp the centre of this eternal kohlu, can we rest.

When I was a student in medical college in 2008, I was going through the same doubts. What is this universe? It doesn't make sense. I met an enlightened person (in my humble opinion) in Rishikesh. I asked him what this was all about.

He said, "If you are sitting under a tree and a snake falls from a branch onto your lap, what will you do? Will you ask yourself - Where has this snake come from? Did someone throw it at me? Is someone trying to kill me, or am I just an unlucky guy?"

No, you won't analyse this. You'll get up in the blink of an eye and throw the snake away.

So, my dear, this world is a snake; it has fallen into your lap. Throw it away. Don't waste your time on analysis. Listen to the masters and throw away the snake first. Then you won't have anything to analyse at all."

That satisfied me. Hope it satisfies you as well.

CHAPTER EIGHT

THREE STATES OF BEING

We have said that waking and dream states are identical and are just appearing and disappearing in consciousness like clouds passing through the clear sky. But what about the third state? The deep sleep. Deep sleep is a universal experience. We all experience deep sleep. Even animals have deep sleep. In fact, deep sleep is a state which is a great equalizer. Every conscious entity has exactly the same deep sleep. Rich, poor, dog, human, sick, healthy - in deep sleep, all identities and physical and mental properties are gone. All that is left is deep, satisfying, energizing deep sleep.

So let us add another cloud in the clear sky of consciousness - waking, dream, and deep sleep.

Some people may say - there is no awareness in deep sleep. But we are always aware of our deep sleep state. Our experience is "I slept. I had a few dreams, but then I had deep sleep and slept peacefully." If we were not aware of our deep sleep phase, we would say "I slept at 10 PM and now it's 6 AM. I don't know what happened in between." But that's not what we report, we are aware of the deep sleep phase even though there was no object, thought or feeling. It's wrong to say "there is no consciousness in deep sleep." In fact, there is ONLY consciousness in deep sleep. Out of the trio of known, knower, and knowledge, there is only the knowledge aspect but no known or knower.

So all three states - waking, dream and deep sleep - are just passing through the consciousness which is our own true SELF. All three states come and go. All are false. Unchanging consciousness is the true state, and that is the real you.

Other states like coma, trance, and drug-induced states are not common experiences. Not everybody has a mystical experience. Here, we are talking about our everyday, verifiable personal experiences. We are being rational and objective. But eventually, if someone pushes it, these unusual states would also fall within the waking category. Even a mystical state can only be experienced in waking or dream state. The states are secondary, consciousness is primary.

CHAPTER NINE

TRADITIONAL EXAMPLES TO EXPLAIN THE SELF

The world exists inside the self. But the self lies beyond the world, time, space and language. We experience/know other things, circumstances and events with our senses, equipment, theories or calculations. But the self cannot be known or objectified in the same sense.

We gather that we, as individual persons, are like dream characters. We are part of a dream and just like a man in a dream feels the dream world is real, we feel this world is also real, although it isn't. It's all an appearance in consciousness. So the big question is - can we really know the Self? The consciousness in which this dream is playing out?

The answer is NO.

Just like a man in a dream can never know the dreamer, we as individual conscious entities cannot know the Self.

So, does it mean I can never know the Self?

But the Self is more than known. It is always known. In fact, it is me, our own self.

The primary reason we cannot know the self is because there is no need to. I am the Self already. A man in a dream is nothing but the dreamer himself.

But practically speaking, there is an issue. There is a thin veil of error which needs to be removed.

To overcome this unique challenge, there are some traditional examples which we will touch upon.

However, no example is perfect and complete. They cannot be perfect in this case - because we are trying to objectify the subject. When we are using these examples, please note that a specific example is meant to drive home a specific point only. We cannot unnecessarily elaborate the example for the sake of arguments. There are other examples to drive home another point. But still no single example can completely explain the self.

First and my favourite example is The dream state. We have already discussed it in detail. We will take it as the standard template and keep discussing it here and there.

ROPE AND SNAKE

When I was in my hostel in 2007, I remember walking to the hostel mess on a rainy monsoon evening. I saw a large frog sitting in my way, still and quiet. I was taken aback and stood staring at it for a while. I moved closer and suddenly realized it wasn't a frog. It was a couple of banyan leaves arranged in a peculiar fashion. That day I really understood this example.

It goes like this.

Suppose there is a rope in a dark corner. A person walks in and gets scared – oh there is a snake! He jumps away and looks for a stick. Then another man comes and says that's not a snake, it's a flower garland. Another one says it's a wire. But then someone switches on the light. Suddenly they realize it's the rope in its real sense – that's not a snake. What a relief!!

So here, the rope did not create the snake. The rope didn't change into a snake. The problem is not in the rope but rather in the observer. The problem is - first, there is ignorance of the fact that it is a rope, second, there is a false projection of a snake onto the rope.

The rope is not the cause of the snake. If you ask the rope, "why did you change into a snake?", the rope would say: "What snake? What are you talking about? There is no snake."

There is superimposition of falsehood upon the truth. **It is a mixture of real and unreal,like we discussed earlier.** The long, wavy shape of the rope is real, but the visualization of a nonexistent snake in that wavy rope is unreal. This superimposition is a strange phenomenon.

Another thing we see is that **truth is one but the errors are many**. The rope is one, but superimpositions can be many depending on the observer.

Problem is with the observer, not the observed. When the conscious infinite entity observes itself, the process of observation itself causes an error. That error is peculiar, with a strange mixture of error and truth.

The solution is to this error is knowledge (which always hits in a flash). Knowledge that was already there in the person, the person knows how a rope looks like. But this knowledge of the rope gets covered by darkness (absence of light in this case).

Mirage in a Desert

Suppose a tourist YouTuber is wandering in the Thar Desert. He is lost and walking through a hot, dry desert without water. He looks afar and sees a large pond of pristine, clear water. He goes to the place but finds nothing but sand.

This water he saw was not real; it was just an illusion. Nothing was created, it was all a game played by his senses in a peculiar set of surroundings - hot, dry air and sand.

But once he understood that this visible water is not real, it will not tempt him.

When mirage is understood as an illusion, the existence of mirage is falsified but it is still visible to the eyes. So we say that budhijanit gyan is superior to indriyajanit gyan.

This universe which we experience is like a mirage. Just like mirage water appears in sand, this universe appears in consciousness. It is visible to us, no doubt, but it's not real. Once we know the truth, it will still be visible, but we will know its reality and won't be tempted or depressed by it.

Water and waves

In the vastness of the ocean, there are many waves and bubbles. They are nothing but water. A wave has no distinct identity other than water.

Just because the wave has a name, form and function, it doesn't mean it has turned into petrol. The reality of waves and bubbles is water only.

From the point of view of a wave, if it considers itself to be a wave – it is definitely a wave. But if the wave considers itself to be water? Of course it is water only. In fact, the identity of a wave being water is more fundamental because a wave may crash, vanish and disappear, but water is permanent and omnipresent. Water has no fear of being broken, no jealousy of being a small wave, no fear of being evaporated. Even if it evaporates, it is still water. Water is immortal, while a wave is a tiny and depressed mortal entity. **It is up to the wave what it wants to identify with.**

So, as individuals, if we consider ourselves as small conscious entities, fearful, competitive, and full of diseases, we are. But if we consider ourselves as the all-pervading consciousness in which all beings and events are happening, we are that also.

Wave is not conscious, doesnt matter what it believes or knows. **But good thing is we are conscious!!!**

That's your CHOICE. That is - what you think is what you become in a real sense. This effect may not matter much in day-to-day things, but when we talk about our consciousness, it makes a gigantic impact.

Gold and Ornaments

A lady is wearing a necklace, bangles, and earrings made of gold. All these three elements are nothing but gold.The truth is gold only. The money is paid for gold. The ornaments are definitely useful – they have a form, name, and use, no doubt about that. But their only value is the gold itself.

Name, form, and use are changing, they can be melted and changed to something else. If you take away the gold, will a shadow bangle exist? Will there be an outline of a bangle or a cloudy dreamy bangle if gold is removed? When you buy a gold biscuit, do you pay for gold or just the name and shape of the biscuit? The biscuit can be of gold or Parle G. Will you pay the same for both biscuits?

Suppose there is a child who doesn't know what gold is. But he has seen his mother wearing the ornaments. Now his mother calls him one day "Go get me all the gold from the cupboard" the child returns and says there is no gold. Mother is astonished - what? Where is the gold? Now she rushes to check and finds all the jewelry is lying safe.

On asking, the child says - yes, I saw the bangles and necklace, but I didn't see the gold. Now, this childish but serious mistake takes place because the child has no knowledge about gold. His knowledge and focus is solely on name and form.

A marine scientist sees the ocean as a body of water, whilst a surfer has his focus on the waves only. However, water remains the same.

From the point of view of gold, if a necklace is melted, the gold is safe and sound. But from a necklace's point of view, if it is melted, its entire existence would be lost.

The necklace was only gold, it just got attracted to its name and form and forgot its true nature. It was stuck to its individuality. It will suffer for that mistake if not corrected. It will be melted and destroyed. Its always better for a necklace to realise and stick to its Gold Identity if it wants to avoid disaster.

CHAPTER TEN

HOW DO THE AWAKENED LIVE?

Once a normal person awakens, the dream state disappears in an instant. The entire existence of the dream world is falsified.

But to an Self Awakened person, the waking world keeps appearing. But since he is now merged with consciousness (which transcends the waking state), the entire waking state appears like a dream – like a movie is playing in front of an observer. Like a mirage, the world appears to him but no longer attracts him, because he knows the reality behind that appearance.

A dream exists in the past. But for the truly awakened person, even the ongoing waking state appears like a dream right in the present. His bias of presence is gone.

For an awakened person, the three states come and go like clouds in a clear sky, like channels changing on a TV. The consciousness (in which the person has now merged) is untouched by these states.

PERSONALITY

The awakened is not a person anymore. He has nothing to do with his personality, ego or world. He is as much attached to his body as he is attached to a bird flying in the sky. For him, all beings are the same.

All beings exist inside him like a dream exists inside a dreamer. Everything is one, everything is his own self. He realizes that everything is "appearing" in himself.

He will not say "I know this consciousness that you are talking about." He would say - "I am the consciousness."

ONENESS AND LOVE

In my dream, everything is me.

The dog, cars, trees, sky, and people are me only. So, does the awakened see this in real time. For us, it's a concept, but for the awakened, it's an ever-present reality. For them, all bodies are inside them just like all dream bodies are inside a dreamer. They have a feeling of 'I' for all entities in the waking world. They know for a fact that consciousness is the only thing existing here. All other entities, including their own body and mind, are just appearances in consciousness. They love a stranger like their own personality, they love a dog likewise. For them, all entities are one and exist in their self, the singular consciousness. The differences are just superficial.

BEHAVIOUR

Now you may ask, if everything is one in that enlightened state, even a dog and a teacher are one reality. You touch the feet of your teacher as a sign of respect. Will he also touch the feet of a dog? If all are one reality and there is no difference, why doesn't an enlightened person touch the feet of a dog also? Why does he prostrate only in front of his teacher?

It's true that everything is one reality but the instruction by teachers is – samdrishti, not samvyavhar - You see everything as One but you don't behave like that. In the practical world, even after knowing all this is One consciousness, the awakened will behave absolutely morally and in accordance with the ethics of society. That's very important. The behaviour of awakened individuals is like everyone else's.

However it's also true that the enlightened have no obligation to follow the rules of the world because they don't exist in the world; the world exists inside of them. There is no obligation to the dream world for the dreamer, who is always free from the dream. It is said even if the Awakened destroys the world , he will not be faulted. Does anyone blame you for destroying your own daydream?

An enlightened person only **acts** like a human. They are beyond time, space, and events, having merged with primordial consciousness. But still, they act and behave like a common person out of their own generosity and safety.

ACTING FOR FUN

Imagine a person wandering in a desert. He notices a mirage far away and hope to access some water. However, upon reaching there, he realised that it's actually an illusion . His desire and effort to achieve that water will dissipate. He has known the truth of mirage.

Now imagine a group of his friends also arrive there and all of them are excited to see the mirage water. Everyone is jumping with joy – water, water!! Now the realized person knows the truth behind the so-called water, but still, he plays along for fun (fun sake – Vinod matra vyavhaar). He would **ACT** as if he is ignorant. He would joyfully go with them, even carrying an inflated bed to swim in the water. He is fully aware but just having fun.

Sometimes, Nakal is better than Asal (acting is better than real). A man is stressed and sad in reality, but Amitabh Bachchan is playing sad and stressed in a movie. I bet Amitabh will look more genuine and convincing than a real person in the same situation.

Just like a prince goes incognito, living as a beggar in his kingdom. He is behaving like a beggar, eating like a beggar, and suffering like a beggar outwardly. But deep inside, he knows he is the prince of the same kingdom. He may act like he is suffering, but his suffering is fake because he knows he is not a beggar but a prince. He will feel the **joy of acting** more than he will feel the suffering of being a beggar. **For him, joy is inward and deep, and suffering is outward and superficial.**

This is how person who is a knower of truth behaves and has fun in this world. Indians call him Jivanmukt.

POWER.

Since he is beyond time and space and the entire universe exists in him, does it mean that he can control this universe? Can he make changes in time and space? Can he cure an incurable disease? **Can he make a cow fly?**

Technically, YES!! He can.

Just like in your daydream, you are the creator and controller of your entire daydream. The daydream exists inside you. Everything in your daydream is YOU yourself. YOU are the all-powerful controller of your dream. When the enlightened man becomes one with the Pure Consciousness, he can very well make changes in the waking state just like YOU can make changes in your daydream.

But there is one condition. He must have a very focused and pure mind. Enlightened men in history have been of two kinds – those who haven't done any mental or psychic control during the preparatory stage and those who have. **The latter can definitely make changes in the time-space matrix, which we would normally call miracles.** But it's nothing miraculous. It's as simple as making changes in your daydreams.

But normally, such awakened individuals won't have any desire to change anything.

Would you ever want to make any effort to win a lottery in a dream? Will you throw a reception party for a wedding that happened in a dream? Would you run away from bullets fired from a TV screen?

Why bother with something if it's not true? If it's all fake, making any such effort is not just futile but also makes you the butt of jokes in your own eyes.

Therefore, most enlightened people will not make any changes to the Universal laws, even if they have the ability to do so. They will only teach and guide others towards consciousness, which is the ultimate truth.

GUIDANCE.

For any person, the only place where consciousness can be experienced is their own self, not anywhere external. So the enlightened will guide them inside, not outside. Only for very extroverted people, they will guide them outside and bring them around to the inner self in due course of time.

Every now and then, such masters can perform miracles or make changes in the time-space matrix, but only for a single purpose - the welfare of others, out of compassion and mercy.

Fate and suffering.

As consciousness, he is no longer bound by any rules and regulations, but his body will continue to behave and exist according to past habits and tendencies. He is no longer identified with his body-mind unit. But this body-mind unit will suffer according to the physical laws of nature. If a tree falls on his body, the body will be crushed. If a tiger bites his body, he will bleed. Enlightenment doesn't mean his body won't suffer like others. The only benefit is he is not attached to his body and its suffering. He will feel the suffering in the same way as he would feel the suffering of a flying bird. The body-mind paradigm is left way below his relevance.

CHAPTER ELEVEN

REAL LIFE PRACTICES – HOW TO DESTROY THE ILLUSION!!

Alright, we are now convinced that This consciousness is the only reality. But we can't ignore the fact that I as a small human still exist and I am troubled by ups and downs. How can I ignore that which is a practical reality to me , though it may all be an appearance. I also understand that the only way to get rid of suffering and eternal joy is to Wake up from this dream like illusion .

So what should I do practically to end this dream and break out of this time space matrix. How to be the Neo?

For this , three things are necessary. we can only experience CONSCIOUSNESS within us with the faculty of **intuition**. There is no external agency which can help us here. To achieve this , we must have 3 qualities

1. Purity of mind
2. Introvert mind
3. Focussed mind

We won't go into detail into each of this . Let's just discuss how to achieve this stage. Also You don't have to follow any religion or texts to achieve this. Truth doesn't depend on religion.

A. **Truth**

First and foremost condition to achieve the three qualities is to Follow TRUTHFULNESS in daily life. It's non negotiable.

During MBBS ,I had a senior who lived next door to me in my hostel.

He had taken a pledge of speaking truth "I will not speak a lie and I will not do anything which makes me speak a lie to coverup in future. Even if I have to die or go to jail."

I have seen him up close and personal. During exams, many times there were very tough questions which were post graduate level. Some students cheated and examiners turned a blind eye just to let the students pass. But he never cheated. He left the answer sheet blank but he never cheated.

Infact he never made any kind of promise (Sankalp nahi karunga , he would say) . Once I asked him . Sir let's go to my home in Sangrur, It's only an hour away . He said ok we will see, if it happens we will go. He didn't promise me. He said that I never make any promise because if I am unable to keep that promise ,I will be declared a liar.

He spent most of his time doing Pranayam, Kushti and Chanting of Om Namah Bhagvate Vasudeva mantra. He had six-pack abs and an amazing infectious laugh. He was simplicity at its best. Always wore very simple slippers and pant shirt. Not even a belt. He didn't study much but whatever he used to read , the same questions would appear in the exam next day. Once a surgery viva was going on for final exam. He got a case of obstructive jaundice . He didn't know a few answers. He simply told the examiner "sir I don't know this answer." To everyone's surprise, the examiner himself started explaining and passed him.

I lived there for 3 years He was so much established in truth that he had aced it. If by mistake he would say " looks like it will rain today". Then it was sure it would rain. He had somehow achieved that Vak Siddhi .

Such level of truth is needed to break this illusion. Not everyone can do that. But I have met people who are doing it in this age and times.

Knowledge only grows with respect. I mean to say Its important to respect your knowledge .If the world is an appearance in consciousness, not real – why would you lie? If you don't respect your Knowledge , you cannot reach the self. Knowledge IS Self. On one hand we say – all is fake and on other hand we cheat and lie to get some money. Both cant work together.

A. Non Violence

Second non negotiable thing needed is non Violence. Since everything is your own self, you can't be angry or violent with anyone. Anything bad happening to you, you have to tolerate it like an act of fate or past bad karma.

Another interesting story from life of my senior. He strictly followed non-violence. So much so that there were many mosquitoes in our hostel ground floor where we lived. He never used anything to kill mosquitoes. He would say "let the mosquitoes bite me. I will die but I will not compromise on my principles." He was a Vishnu Devotee . He would always quote the Gita verse " Those who have surrender their life into Me , I will take care of their Yoga and Kshema ". The consciousness in which this entire universe and millions of galaxies exist , would that stay away from protecting me? Lord Vishnu never falls behind in protecting his devotees. That was his firm resolve. I have seen first hand his resolve to follow all yogic principles of Yama and Dama.

And I have seen the result in a year or so, mosquitoes stopped biting him. Mosquitoes would bite everyone , but never bit him. He had achieved the Ahimsa Siddhi .

C. **No cheating or Bad Earning**

Always work honestly to the best of your ability in your professional and personal life. Never expect anything. Even if something bad happens, keep doing the good work as long as you yourself are satisfied that you are doing the right thing. The light of knowledge will soon shine inside.

Whenever we would go out to eat. Sometimes I would sometimes pay for his dinner if he didn't carry money. He always tried to pay me back and I refused. So he would put the due money in my book or slide under my door without telling me.

Another doctor I met recently who followed the principles of Karma Yoga and Honesty. We discussed how to follow these principles when you are a doctor in a corporate hospital. His method was - Everytime he consults a patient , he puts a small candy in a jar as an offering/ reminder and then distribute to kids.

We discussed how many times despite being honest and careful about our treatment, patients may still blame us or say bad things about us. Many times the disease doesn't get better or may need surgery. People may blame or doubt you , but you should never have any bad feelings towards them. Our only duty is to do honest and good work. Consciousness is the ultimate witness. Honest work (karma yoga) is the quickest route to the Ultimate Prize.

D. **BREATH CONTROL**

Breath control or Pranayam is a very powerful tool. Lot said on this topic.

E. **DIET**

Stop all spicy, non veg and intoxicant, stimulant foods. Eat less , keep empty . Cook food yourself if possible. When you eat food, imagine " Consciousness is the cook, consciousness is the food , Consciousness is the eater. Consciousness is the body , Consciousness is the Hunger . Everything is appearing and acting in consciousness "

Take up practice of Weekly fasting or one-time meal etc as suitable. Food has most profound effect on mind.

F. Always have a **smile** on your face. Whenever you remember, smile. Happiness is very strong enabler in this journey. It increases satva like nothing else.
G. **Behaviour** - Speak less, low and slow. Listen and Smile. Dont be opinionated. You dont need to prove your intelligence to anyone. Thats a sign of inferiority complex. Don't act or talk oversmart. Be simple.

Whats the purpose of Talking, Debating or drawing conclusions in a dream...dont even talk about spirituality... Its all fake dream... Do you ever waste time trying to change/improve the dream once you wake up?

The behaviour should be in accordance with the knowledge.

H. **Physical exercise and Nature walk...** Do moderate physical exercise for half hour. Then go for walk among trees and grass.

A. Have mercy on animals and plants.

J. Donate your time and honestly earned money to deserving people. In India, Honest work (karma yoga) is given much more importance than Charity (dan). If you are doing your duty honesty you don't really need to make donations. But still donating and helping needy people is a great way to fasten the journey

K. Read Spiritual books as per your interest and Spiritual stage. This whole discussion we just had was based on Mandukya Upanishad along with my own inputs and experiences. For further reading - I would recommend The Gita, Yogavasishta, Ashtavakra Gita, Panchdashi. **These texts are not religious texts**. They are ultimate works of Psychology, metaphysics and I would dare to say – Physics. Listen to them from qualified teachers. Reading books is not helpful most of the times because we will interpret them based on **our own limited understanding**. Listening to explanations from teachers is much more helpful. Book can never replace teacher.

AX. If you are lucky to find an Enlightened person , go ,serve and spend some time with him. But don't be too involved with works of organizations.

ALL. Focussing the Mind. Try to focus the mind on a single thought or no thought at all. Both are effective. You can either use a Mantra to chant or use a thought like " Everything is Consciousness like a dream. I'm not a man in dream, I'm the dreamer itself. Everything exists in me" Repeat this again and again as needed and then quieit. This is called Vichar Marg. It is said that even 3 seconds of this Vichar can do more benefit than lifetimes of hardwork.

However , the mind will definitely wander off here and there. The trick is to again and again Catch the wandering mind and bring it to same thought /mantra. It's a fight against the mind and ultimately Consciousness will win. It has to because mind is secondary.

N. Visit places where awakened people have lived or meditated. They have real powerful vibes and settle the mind effortlessly.
O. Prayer.

Didn't you say earlier that No matter what he does but a man in dream can never know the dreamer!! That's true. A man in dream cannot know the dreamer.

But dreamer definitely knows the dream man and dream world. Dreamer can do whatever he wants.

The best thing for a seeker is that the Ultimate Reality is Conscious and its also our own Self. So it responds to prayer.

If we, as humans, listen to a person repeatedly requesting us, why won't the Self also listen to our prayers? Afterall it is conscious right, not wood or stone?

In India, consciousness is considered the Ultimate reality of universe. Those who think Indians worship Stones or Statutes are badly mistaken. Indians don't worship the Stone, they worship the Consciousness that exists throughout; like dreamer exists throughout the dream. A mother doesn't love the body of her child, she loves the conscious entity that pervades it. If she loved the body only, even dead bodies would be loved. Its not the statue that is prayed to , It's the Consciousness in Divine Statue that is worshipped. And it does respond for honest and sincere seekers. This Conscious entity is all powerful, without limits.

Also this consciousness is our own Self. We don't have to go anywhere to pray. Its an inside job.

With our effort, we cannot know it ,but we can create an **emotional or situational upheaval** where the Consciousness responds . When do we wake up from a dream? Usually when something terribly good or bad is happening. Something that shakes us. With our effort, we can only shake the Consciousness but it's the grace of consciousness alone which wakes us up.

Apologies

I must apologise for any mistake. Learned people should kindly forgive me for any errors. Im not an author and this is my first ever book. This book was written in a state of flow, I was jotting down the thoughts arising in my mind. Im a very busy surgeon but deeply interested in this topic since my school time. Most of this book was written when I was in MBBS in year 2005-2008 , I still have the handwritten original manuscript which I read quite often. That was the time when I had some of the most amazing experiences which can only be called miracles.

Being a hardcore science student , I always tried to correlate those experiences with physics and still do. Its an amazingly wonderful field. Like a man in dream can never know the dreamer , we as individual entities cannot know the Self. Science is trying hard to reveal the ultimate reality. But in my humble opinion, its not possible in principle to know Consciousness through time space matrix.

This book is just a scratch on the surface . Im not sure if I will write anything more. But there are many topics which I have not covered. I know there are many errors in the writing. But I didn't have time for the elaborate publishing process. I have to publish it as it is, otherwise it will never see the light of the day.

Im reluctant to share my own personal experiences but they were definitely amazing. Life has been very kind to me that it showed me all her beautiful and amazing sides.

Finally I would encourage you to delve deep into the investigation of your own Self. This strange phenomenon, called the universe , appears and disappears, not in any external entity, but in our own consciousness.

Consciousness cooks up this false but unique experience. How and why? It's natural. It's the inherent nature of consciousness. Just like fire is inherently hot. If it's not hot, fire won't exist. It's the existence of fire itself.

Reality is something in which this time and space can come, expand, contract, and vanish. There is only one thing in your own experience in which such amazing and unique thing can happen - that is Your own Self – consciousness, which is a mystery from the ages.

www.ingramcontent.com/pod-product-compliance
Lightning Source LLC
LaVergne TN
LVHW021201160826
845679LV00024B/2199

* 9 7 9 8 8 9 1 8 6 1 1 5 2 *